# Cleared for Take-off!

Chris Oxlade

**OXFORD**
UNIVERSITY PRESS

Great Clarendon Street, Oxford OX2 6DP

Oxford University Press is a department of the University of Oxford.
It furthers the University's objective of excellence in research, scholarship,
and education by publishing worldwide in

Oxford   New York

Auckland   Cape Town   Dar es Salaam   Hong Kong   Karachi
Kuala Lumpur   Madrid   Melbourne   Mexico City   Nairobi
New Delhi   Shanghai   Taipei   Toronto

With offices in

Argentina   Austria   Brazil   Chile   Czech Republic   France   Greece
Guatemala   Hungary   Italy   Japan   Poland   Portugal   Singapore
South Korea   Switzerland   Thailand   Turkey   Ukraine   Vietnam

Oxford is a registered trade mark of Oxford University Press
in the UK and in certain other countries

Text © Chris Oxlade 2005

The moral rights of the author have been asserted

Database right Oxford University Press (maker)

First published 2005

All rights reserved. No part of this publication may be reproduced,
stored in a retrieval system, or transmitted, in any form or by any means,
without the prior permission in writing of Oxford University Press,
or as expressly permitted by law, or under terms agreed with the appropriate
reprographics rights organization. Enquiries concerning reproduction
outside the scope of the above should be sent to the Rights Department,
Oxford University Press, at the address above

You must not circulate this book in any other binding or cover
and you must impose this same condition on any acquirer

British Library Cataloguing in Publication Data

Data available

ISBN 978-0-19-919849-8

7  9  10  8  6

Printed in China by Imago

Paper used in the production of this book is a natural,
recyclable product made from wood grown in sustainable forests.
The manufacturing process conforms to the environmental
regulations of the country of origin.

**Acknowledgements**

The publisher would like to thank the following for permission to reproduce photographs: Alamy/Coverspot: p13 (top); Alamy/Douglas Fisher: p12; Alamy/The Flight Collection: p16; Alamy/Winston Luzier: p4 (bottom); Alamy/Swerve: p7; Aviation Images: pp21 (bottom), 20 (bottom), 22; Aviation Images/M.Wagner: pp15 (top),17 (top, bottom); Corbis UK Ltd: p11 Corbis UK Ltd/Bettmann: pp5,8 (bottom); Corbis UK Ltd/George Hall: p20/21 (centre); Corbis UK Ltd/John van Hassect: p10; Corbis UK Ltd/Kim Kulish: p6; Corbis UK Ltd/Lester Lefkowitz: p9; Corbis UK Ltd/Alain Nogues: p18; Corbis UK Ltd/Reuters: p19 (top); Corbis UK Ltd/Gavin Wickham/Eye Ubiquitous: p8 (top); Corbis UK Ltd/Yogi, Inc: p21 (top); Getty Images: pp13,19 (bottom); Getty Images/J.Wilds/Stringer: p15 (bottom); Science Photo Library/Samuel Ashfield: p4 (top); Skyscan: p14

Cover photo: BAA Aviation Photo Library

Illustrations by Oxford Designers and Illustrators

# Contents

A pilot's job — 4

Pre-flight checks — 6

Time for take-off — 8

Pilots in control — 10

Above the clouds — 12

Which way? — 14

Emergency landing! — 16

Loop the loop — 18

Flying fast — 20

Eject! Eject! — 22

Glossary — 24

# A pilot's job

Have you ever wondered what it would be like to be a pilot? Have you thought about what a pilot does as a plane takes off, as it cruises through the air, and as it comes in to land? In this book we will fly in the **cockpit** of an airliner to find out. We will also:

- find out about the parts of a plane;
- find out what it is like to fly stunt planes and fighter planes;
- find out about being a pilot in the past.

The cockpit of an airliner

Training in a **simulator**

An airliner is a very complicated machine. Airline pilots spend about three years learning and practising before they are allowed to take charge of a plane full of passengers. They have to be good at maths, science, information technology and geography. They must also work well with others, be good at communicating, and stay calm in an emergency.

## Across the Atlantic

In 1927, an American pilot named Charles Lindbergh flew across the Atlantic Ocean on his own. He flew from New York to Paris without stopping. The flight took 33 hours and 39 minutes. That's nearly a day and a half! Lindbergh had to stay awake all the way, or he might have crashed into the sea.

In a modern airliner the same trip takes just seven hours.

Charles Lindbergh and his plane, the *Spirit of St Louis*

# Pre-flight checks

We are going to follow a flight from Heathrow airport in London to John F. Kennedy airport in New York – flight number TT123. The flight time is six hours. This is the time it takes to get from the terminal in London to the terminal in New York, not just the time in the air. The plane is a Boeing 777, with 350 passengers on board.

There are two pilots on the flight. They are the captain and the co-pilot. While the passengers settle into their seats, the pilots do their pre-flight checks. They check over the plane to make sure all its parts are working properly.

The flight deck of a Boeing 777. The captain sits in the left-hand seat and the co-pilot sits in the right-hand seat.

## Wings and engines

The pilot checks the wings and the engines. When the plane is flying along, air flows over and under the wings. This creates lift, keeping the plane in the air. The flowing air also slows the plane down, so the 777 has two jet engines to push it forwards.

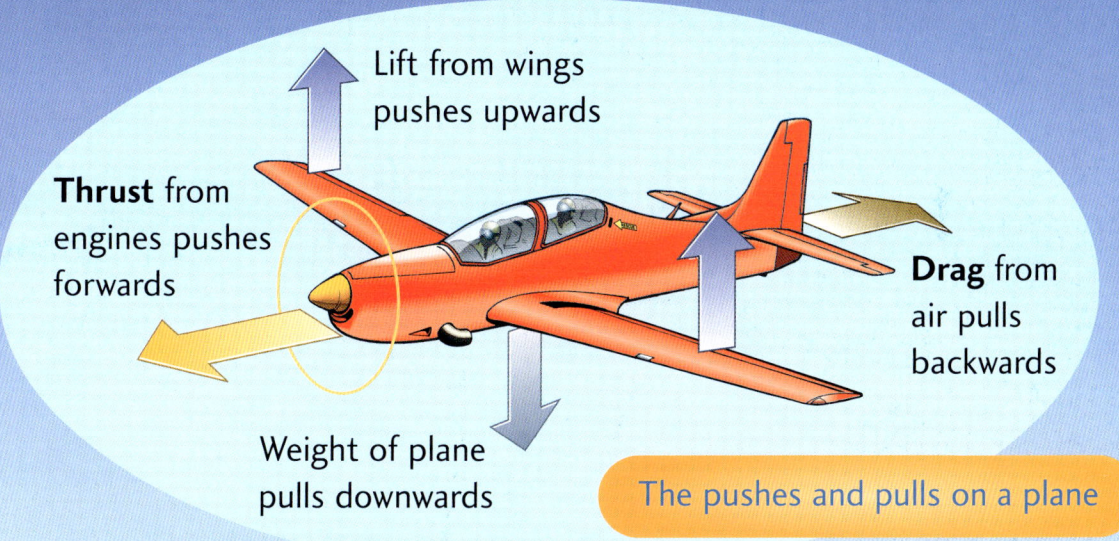

The pushes and pulls on a plane

## Security in the air

Before boarding a plane, passengers go through security checks to make sure they are not carrying any weapons. Security staff check inside bags with X-ray machines. They check people's clothes with electronic scanners. Security is very strict since the terrorist attacks of September 11, 2001. But terrorist attacks on planes are extremely rare.

# Time for take-off

The passengers are in their seats, with their seat belts on. All the doors are tightly closed. The Boeing 777 is ready to begin its flight. The captain starts the **jet engines**. The plane can't reverse, so a truck pushes it backwards from the terminal at Heathrow. It trundles along the **taxiway** to runway 27R, and waits at the **threshold**. It's time for take-off.

The aircraft must take on fuel. The captain tells the ground crew how much is needed.

## Amy Johnson (1903-1941)

British pilot Amy Johnson was on a wartime mission in 1941 when she died in a flying accident. In 1930, she had become the first woman to fly solo from England to Australia. It was a heroic flight. She flew in a tiny biplane called a Gypsy Moth. The journey took 19 days, and she flew over shark-infested water and through high mountain ranges.

Waiting to be cleared for take-off

## Sitting at the threshold

In their radio headphones, the pilots hear instructions from Heathrow **control tower**. 'Tower to 123 Heavy. Cleared for take-off.' The controllers use the word 'Heavy' for large jets like the Boeing 777. This helps to distinguish them from smaller air traffic. The co-pilot pushes the **throttles** forwards. The two giant jet engines begin to roar and the plane speeds down the runway. Soon it's going fast enough to take off. The co-pilot calls 'Rotate'. The captain pulls back on the controls and the 777 climbs steeply into the air over London. After a few seconds the co-pilot pulls a lever to fold away the **undercarriage**.

# Pilots in control

A plane's cockpit is full of levers, switches and buttons that control its parts. In front of each pilot is a **control column**, two foot pedals, and lots of **instruments**. When the pilot pulls the column back the plane climbs. When they push the column forward the plane descends. When they turn the wheel and press the pedals the plane turns left or right.

Captain's control column

Co-pilot's control column

engine throttles

# How fast, how high?

Screens, dials and lights in the cockpit are called instruments. The airspeed indicator shows how fast the plane is going. The **altimeter** (say al-tim-iter) shows how high above the ground the plane is. Other instruments show if the engines and other parts of the plane are working properly. These are all part of what is called the primary flight display.

The primary flight display of a Boeing 777

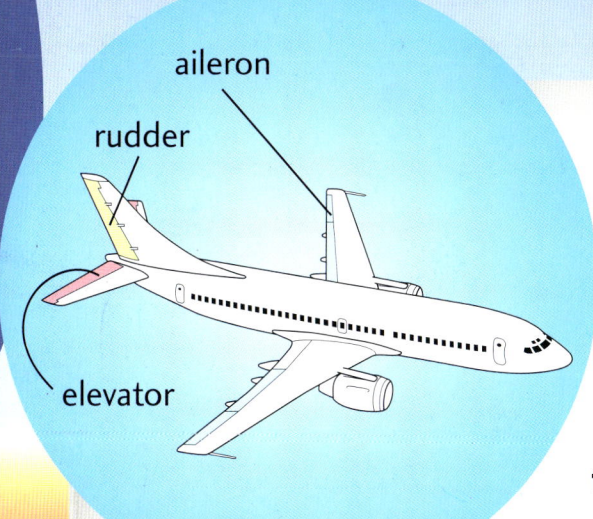

## Control surfaces

The pilot's control column and pedals move parts of the plane called control surfaces. The column moves the **ailerons** on the wings and **elevators** on the **tailplane** up or down. The pedals move the rudder on the **fin** from side to side.

# Above the clouds

After take-off, flight TT123 climbs quickly into the sky. Twenty minutes later it is flying 8,000 metres above the ground and is heading out over the Atlantic Ocean. This is called the cruising **altitude**. It stays up here for most of the flight. Cruising speed is about 900 kilometres per hour. The cabin crew serve a meal to the passengers. After the meal the passengers usually sleep or watch in-flight movies.

Pilots enjoy sunny weather on every flight, even when it's cloudy below!

The pilots switch on the plane's autopilot. This is a computer that flies the plane automatically. It keeps the plane on course and at the correct altitude. Now the pilots can relax for a while. They have a meal and a drink, and tell the passengers about the weather in New York. All the time they keep an eye on the plane's instruments to make sure that everything is working properly.

The two pilots each eat a different meal. This is to reduce the chances of food poisoning.

## Turbulence

Two hours after take-off the Boeing 777 begins to bump up and down, like a car driving on a bumpy road. The cabin crew ask the passengers to sit down and put on their seat belts. The bumping can be frightening, but it is just turbulence. This happens when a plane flies through air that is swirling about. After ten minutes the turbulence disappears again.

Pilots always try to avoid flying through thunderstorms, where turbulence is normally very bad.

# Which way?

How do the pilots of flight TT123 find their way from London to New York? It's dark and cloudy so they can't see the ground, and there are no landmarks in the Atlantic Ocean. The Boeing 777 has electronic gadgets that tell the pilots where the plane is. One of these is **GPS** (Global Positioning System), which many cars have, too. There is also an electronic **compass** that shows which direction the plane is flying in. Finding the way is called navigating.

An airliner has a computer map that shows the ground below.

## Air traffic control

The pilots can't fly wherever they want. They must follow a special route between London and New York so they don't crash into other planes. They are told which route to take by air-traffic controllers in Britain, Ireland, Canada and America. The controllers talk to the pilots by radio. They tell pilots to climb or descend or to change direction.

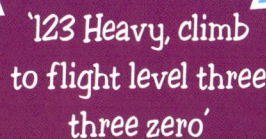

'123 Heavy, climb to flight level three three zero'

The air-traffic controller is asking the pilot to climb to an altitude of 33,000 feet (about 10,000 metres).*

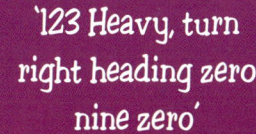

'123 Heavy, turn right heading zero nine zero'

The air-traffic controller is asking the pilot to turn right onto a compass heading of 90 degrees.

* Air-traffic controllers and pilots always use feet rather than metres. They never adopted the metric system.

## Follow the railway

A hundred years ago pilots found their way by following railways and roads between towns. They couldn't fly when it was foggy because they could get lost.

# Emergency landing!

Five and a half hours after take-off, flight TT123 is almost in New York. The pilots reduce engine power. The plane slows and begins to descend. The pilots follow instructions from air-traffic control, and soon the flight is approaching runway 31R at John F. Kennedy airport. The co-pilot lowers the undercarriage. But there is problem! A red warning light shows that the nose wheel has not lowered properly.

Landing is the trickiest part of a flight for the pilots.

The pilots quickly and calmly tell the airport control tower about the problem. They fly slowly over the airport, and the controllers look at the undercarriage through binoculars. Everything looks okay, so the pilots decide to fly round again and attempt to land. Emergency vehicles rush to the runway in case the undercarriage collapses on touchdown.

An airliner about to land. At the back of the wings are flaps. They come out to help the plane to stay in the air at low speed.

## Touchdown

'One hundred feet, seventy-five feet, fifty, forty...' calls the co-pilot as the plane gets closer and closer to the ground. The pilot cuts engine power and the Boeing 777 touches down very gently. The pilots hold their breath, but the nose wheel is fine. The captain puts the engines into reverse thrust, which slows the plane down quickly. The plane turns off the runway and taxis to the airport. Flight TT123 is over.

Emergency vehicles rush to the runway.

# Loop the loop

Stunt pilots fly for fun! They fly rolls, spins and loops at air displays or in stunt-flying competitions. They need lots of skill and lots of practice to do these amazing tricks. Flying sharp turns and tight loops causes a pilot's blood to rush to their head or to their feet, making them feel dizzy. Stunt pilots need padded seats for comfort and super-strong harnesses to stop them from falling out as the plane flies upside down.

*Stunt planes are lightweight and strong, with very powerful engines.*

## The Immelmann

The Immelmann turn is a famous stunt. The pilot does half a loop and then half a roll. It was named after World War I fighter ace Max Immelmann. He invented the turn to escape from enemy fighters.

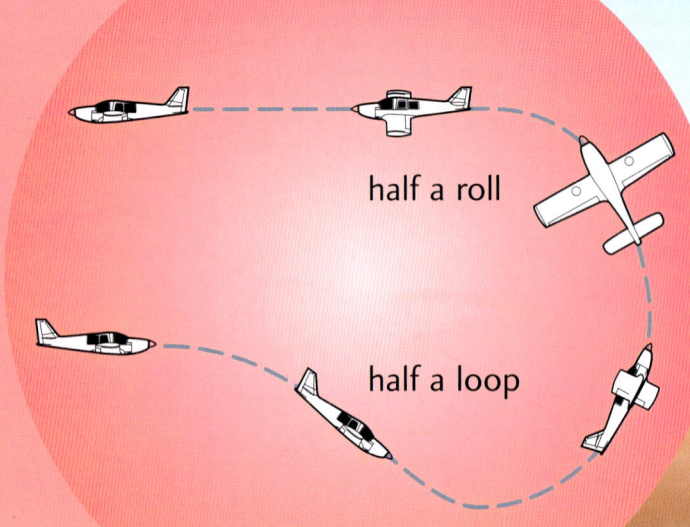

The Red Arrows are a famous stunt-flying team. It takes great skill to fly so close to each other in these fast jets.

## Barnstormers

American stunt pilots of the 1920s were called barnstormers. They earned money with dare-devil flying displays in old World War I planes. Can you think why they were called barnstormers?

# Flying fast

Only the top pilots are allowed to fly fast fighter jets. These planes are super fast. Top speed is twice as fast as a jet airliner. There's no time for fighter pilots to look at the view! As well as flying a plane, they might have to attack enemy fighters with guns and missiles, and escape from enemy fire. They have computers to help fly the plane and to aim the weapons.

## Runway at sea

The trickiest job for a fighter pilot is landing on an aircraft carrier. The deck is very small, and often rolling about because of the waves. A landing officer on the deck tells the pilot to fly to the left or right, or higher or lower, guiding the pilot down safely.

If the pilot judges the landing perfectly, the plane hooks onto a wire that stops it sliding off the deck. If they miss they fly off and try again.

A giant catapult fires planes off the deck. It temporarily pushes the pilot's eyeballs back into the skull!

## Head-up displays

A fighter jet has what is called a head-up display. It lets the pilot see instruments at the same time as looking out of the window.

# Eject! Eject!

Fighter aircraft have seats called ejector seats. If an aircraft goes wrong or is hit by something, the seat hurls the pilot out of the cockpit to safety. The pilot activates the seat by pulling on the ejector handle. The flow chart opposite shows you what happens next. Pilots can eject safely at speeds of more than 2000 kilometres per hour, even if the aircraft is only a few metres off the ground, as in the picture below.

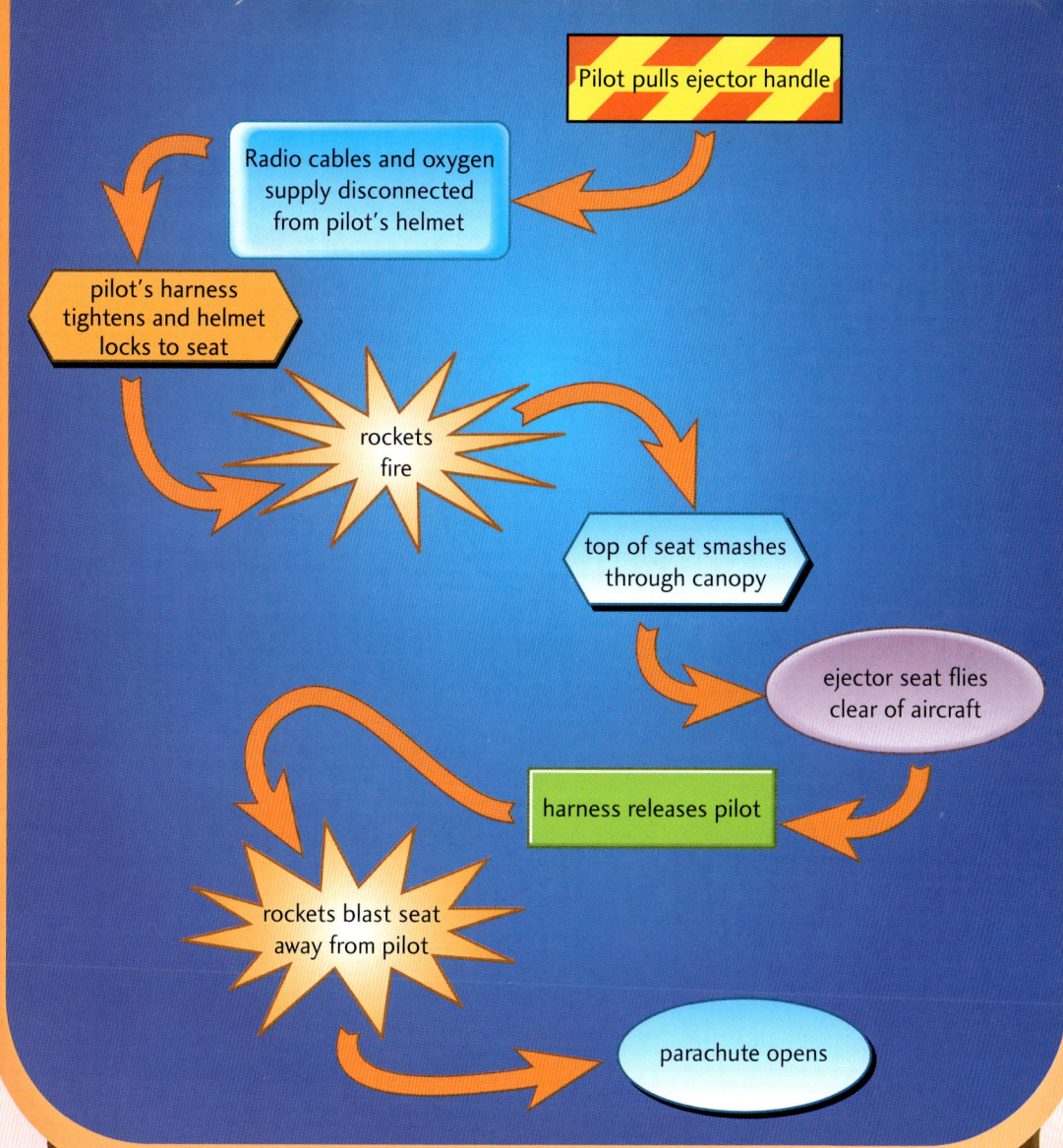

## Ejector seat history

The first ejector seat was tested in 1946. Before this, pilots had to clamber out of their crippled aircraft before parachuting to the ground. The pilots of World War I were not given parachutes. Air-force bosses thought the pilots would jump out if the enemy started shooting at them. What was supposed to happen after this is anyone's guess!

# Glossary

**aileron** – hinged part on the back of the wing. Helps balance the plane

**air-traffic controller** – person who tells planes where to fly

**altimeter** – an instrument that shows the altitude of a plane

**altitude** – height above the sea or the ground

**cockpit** – the place in a plane where the pilot sits. Usually called the flight deck in an airliner

**compass** – a device that shows which way is North, used for finding the way

**control column** – a stick and wheel that a pilot uses to steer a plane through the air

**control tower** – a tower at an aiport from where the movements of all the planes at the airport are controlled

**drag** – a pull made on a plane by the air that tries to slow the plane down

**elevator** – a moveable part that controls the pitch (or angle) of the plane

**fin** – the upright part of a plane's tail

**GPS** – short for Global Positioning System. A GPS machine shows its exact position using radio signals from satellites

**instruments** – screens, dials and lights that give information to the pilots

**jet engine** – an engine that makes a push by sending out a stream of hot gas

**simulator** – a machine on the ground that pilots train in

**tailplane** – small wings at the tail of a plane

**taxiway** – a road that planes use to move between an airport terminal and the runway

**threshold** – the top of a runway

**throttle** – a control used to change the thrust made by an engine

**thrust** – the push made by a plane's engines

**undercarriage** – wheels that a plane uses to roll along the ground